Beautiful Butterflies

DESIGNS WITH A SPLASH OF COLOR

JESSICA MAZURKIEWICZ

DOVER PUBLICATIONS, INC.
MINEOLA, NEW YORK

Traditionally one of the most interesting and enchanting coloring motifs, the beautiful butterfly graces the pages of this attractive collection. Use your imagination to add color to the vivid patterns on each pair of exquisite wings and to the elaborate backgrounds containing everything from flowers and fruit, to abstract shapes and patterns. This eye-catching collection by artist Jessica Mazurkiewicz includes thirty-one plates of charming butterfly designs that will delight artists of all ages. Plus, perforated pages make displaying your finished work easy!

Bibliographical Note

Beautiful Butterflies: Designs with a Splash of Color, published by Dover Publications, Inc., in 2016, is a republication of the plates from *Beautiful Butterfly Designs,* originally published by Dover in 2009.

International Standard Book Number

ISBN-13: 978-0-486-80777-5
ISBN-10: 0-486-80777-0

Manufactured in the United States by RR Donnelley
80777001   2016
www.doverpublications.com

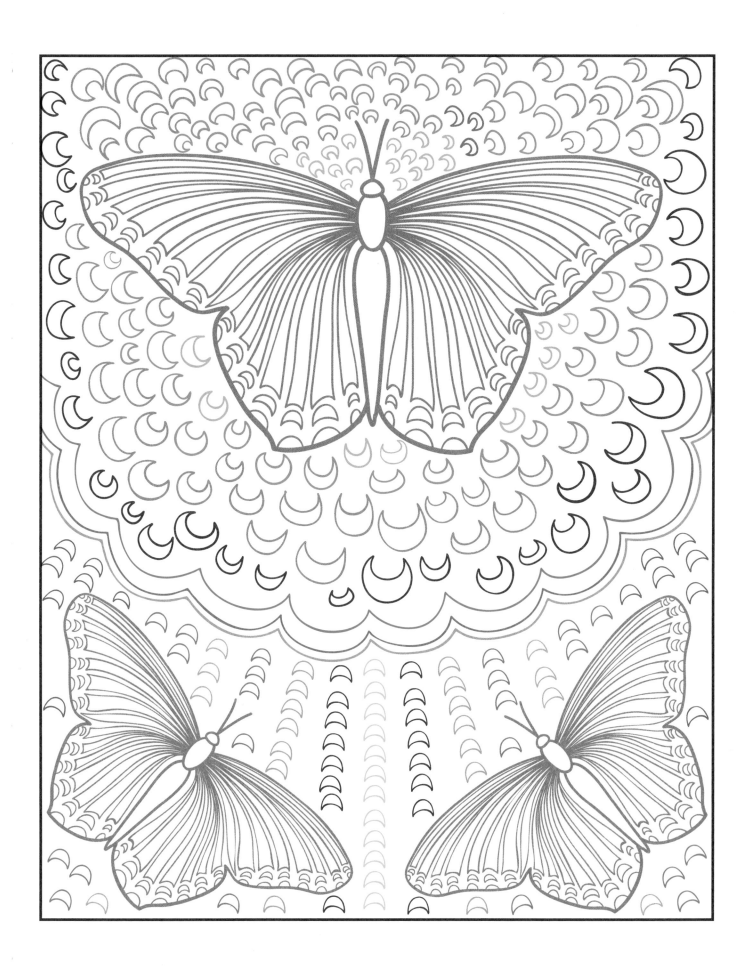

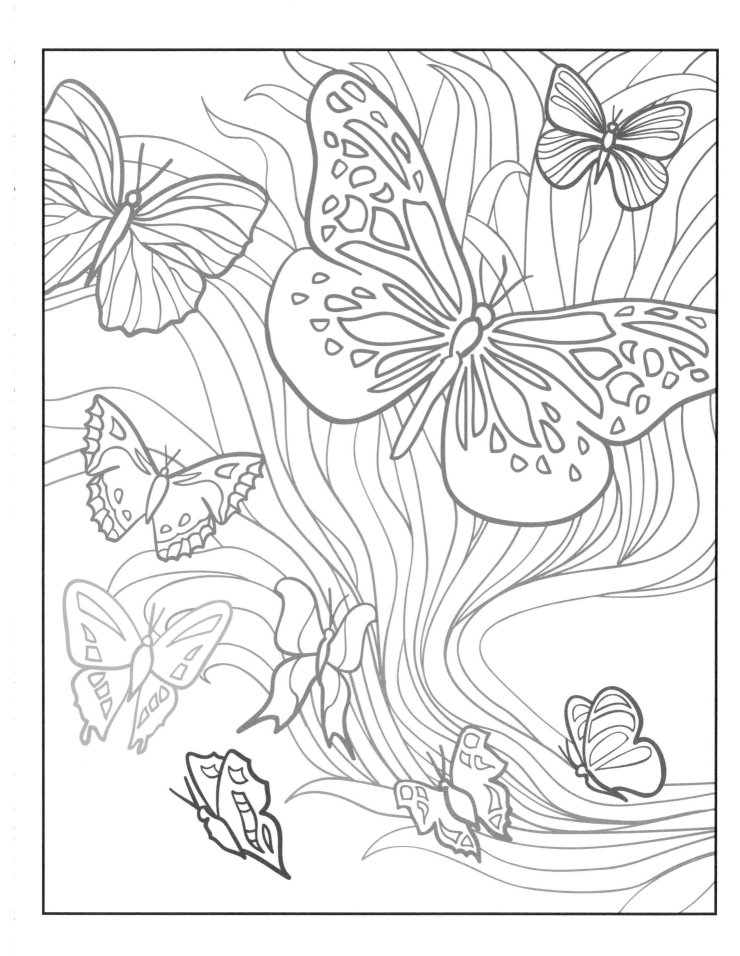

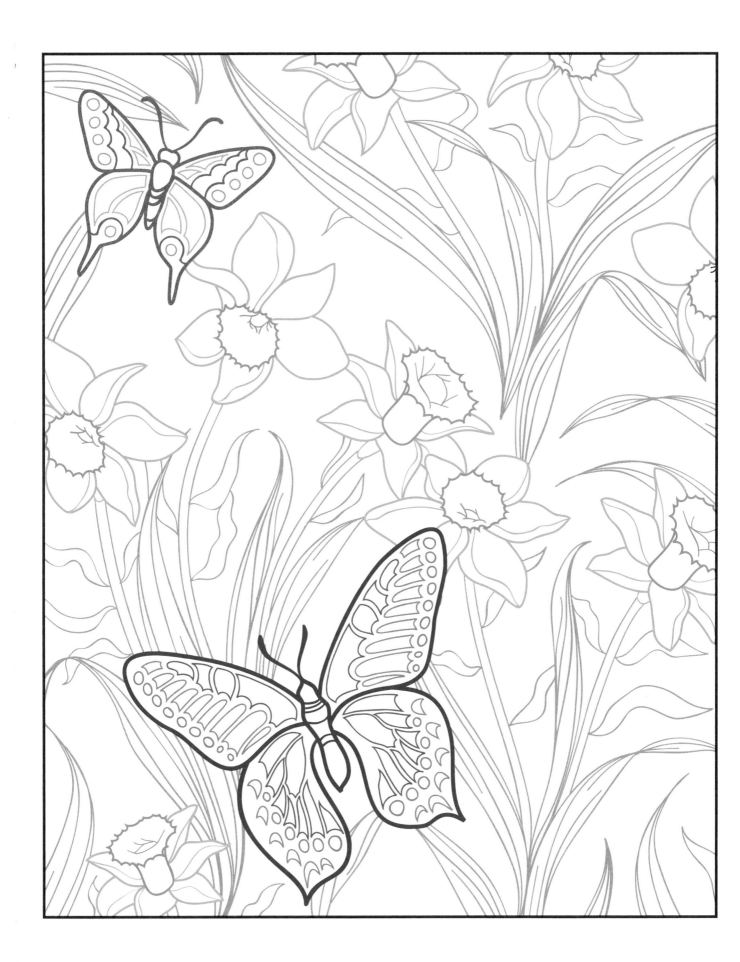

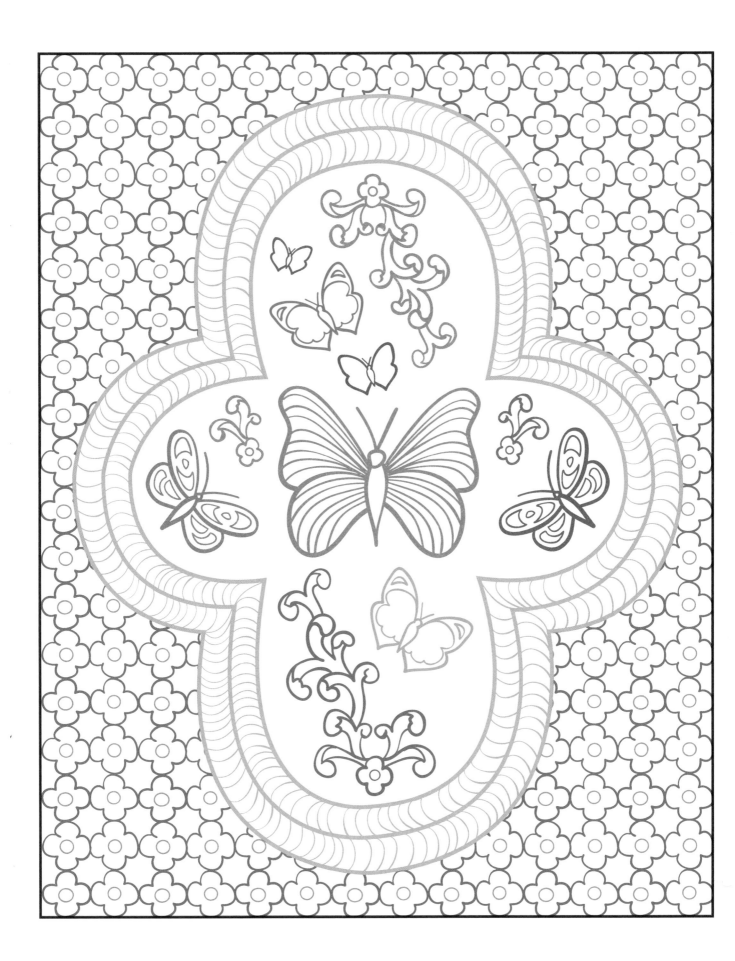

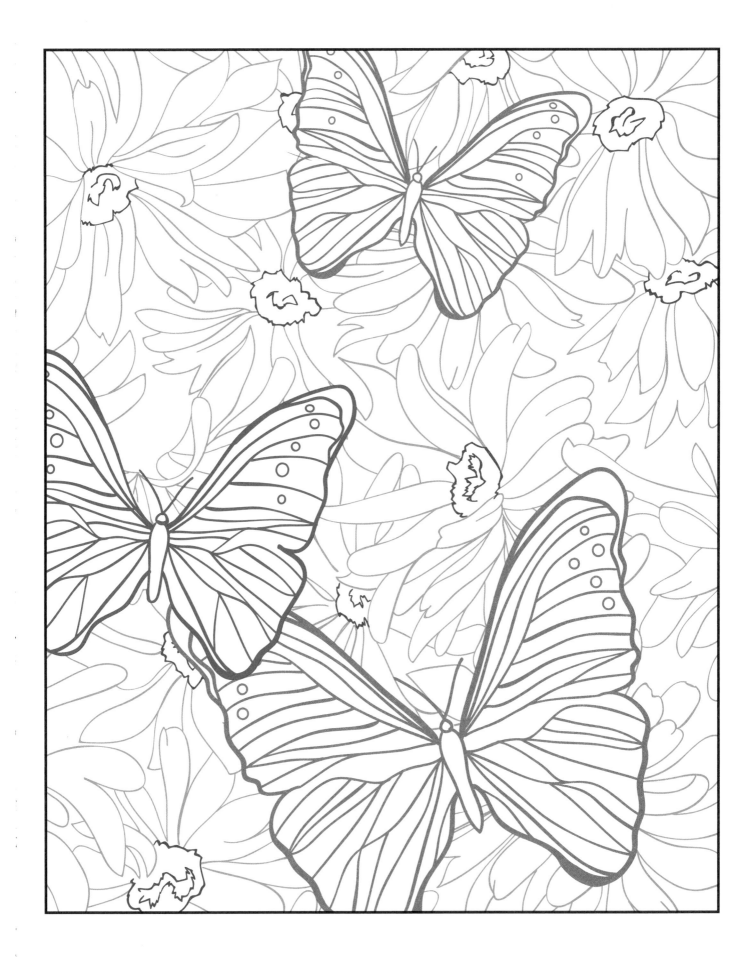

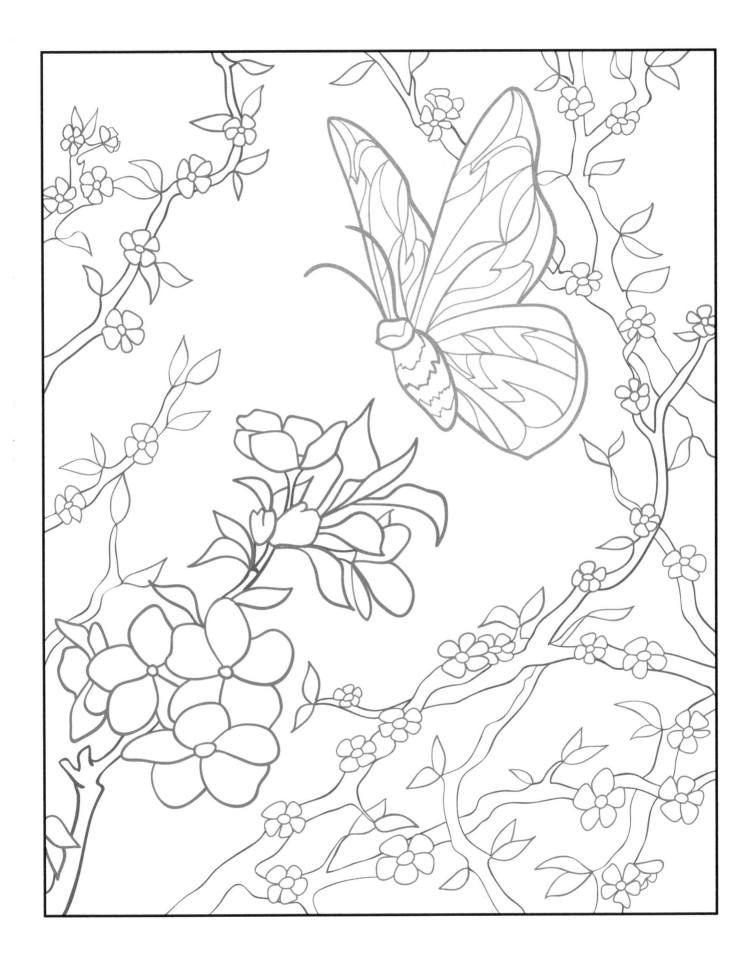

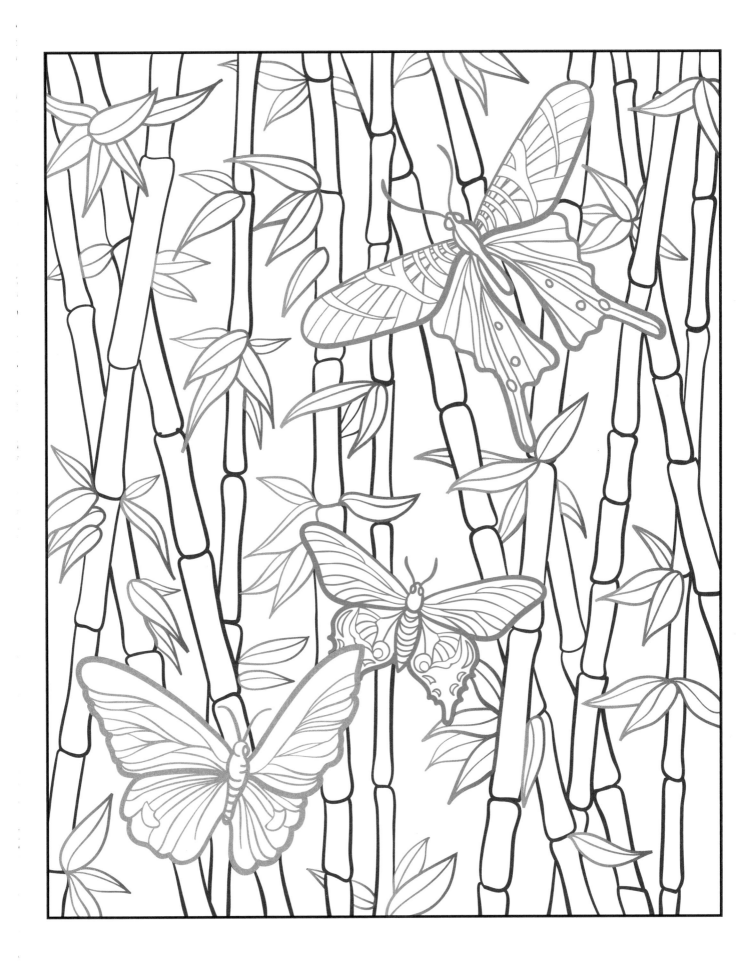

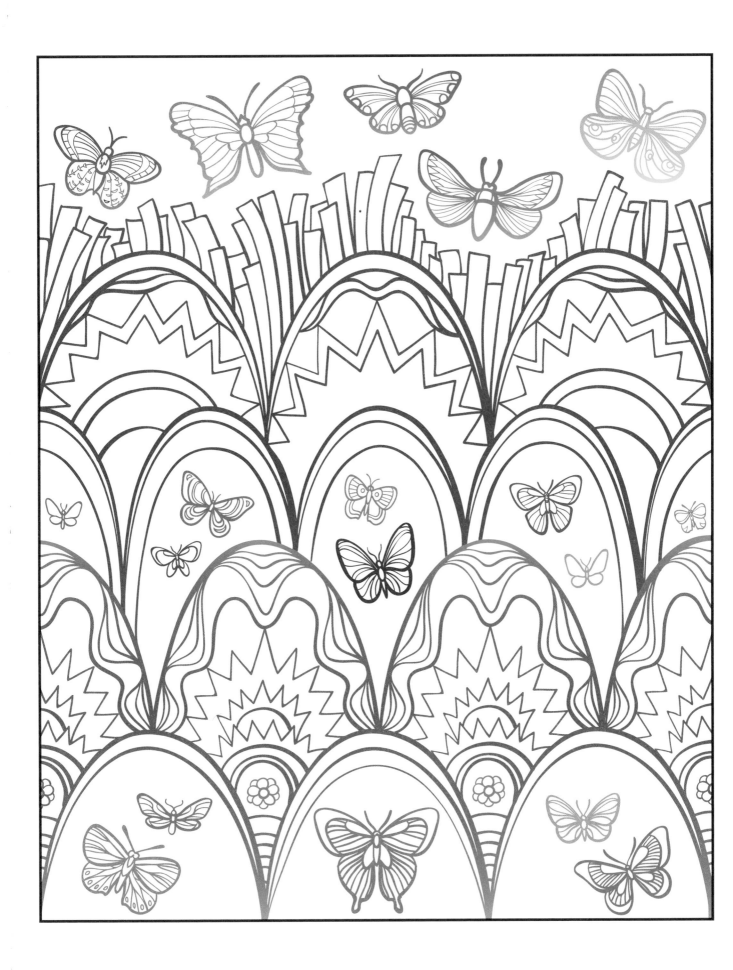

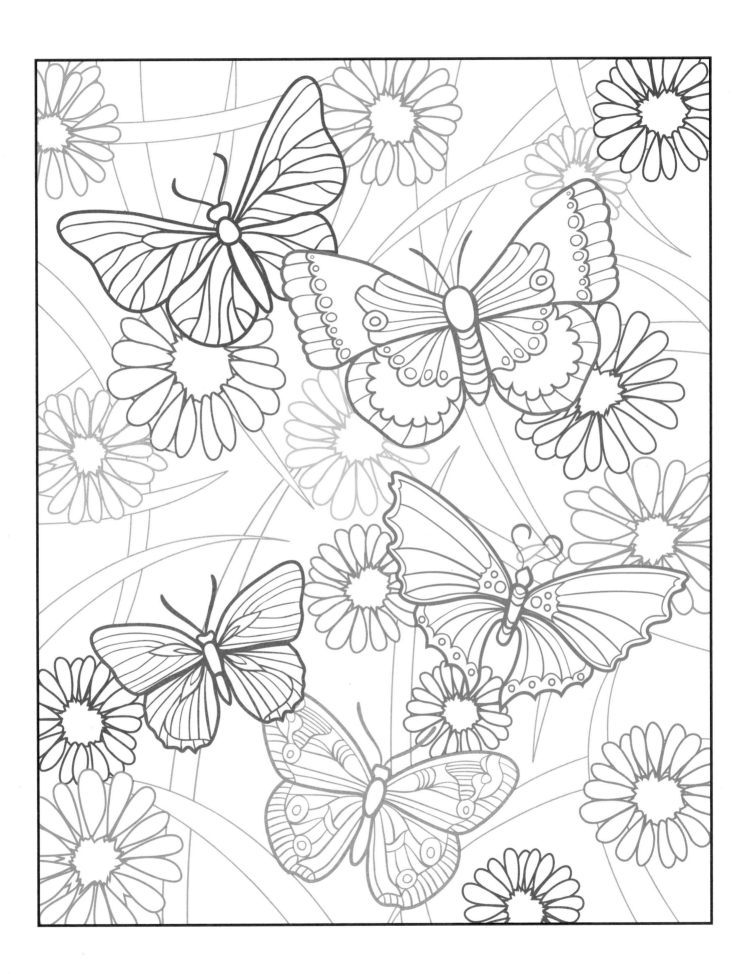

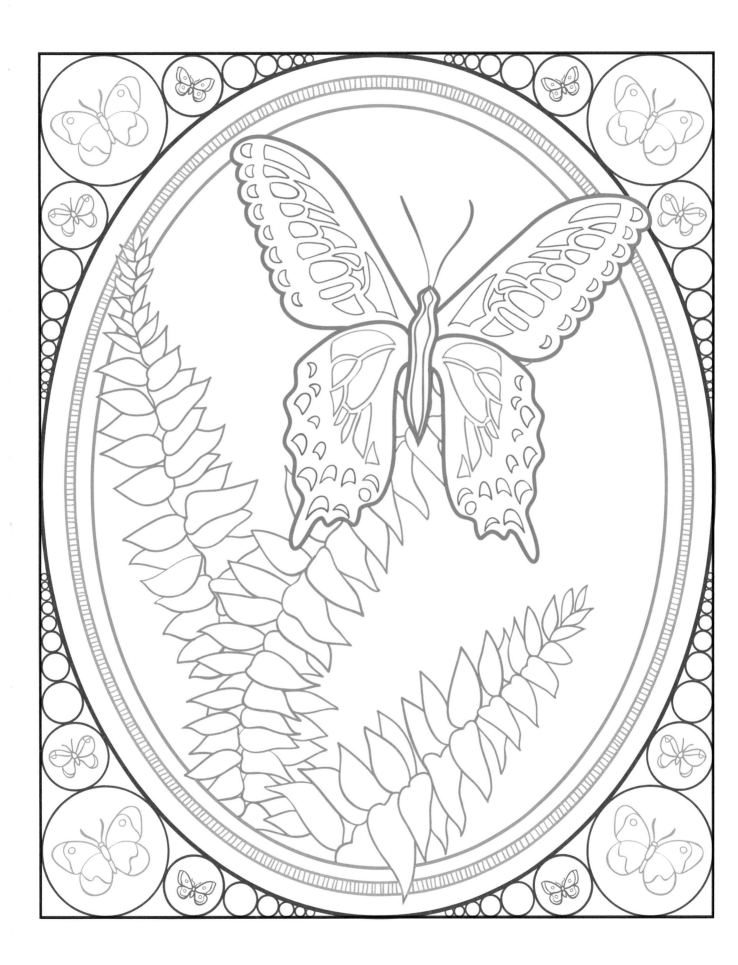

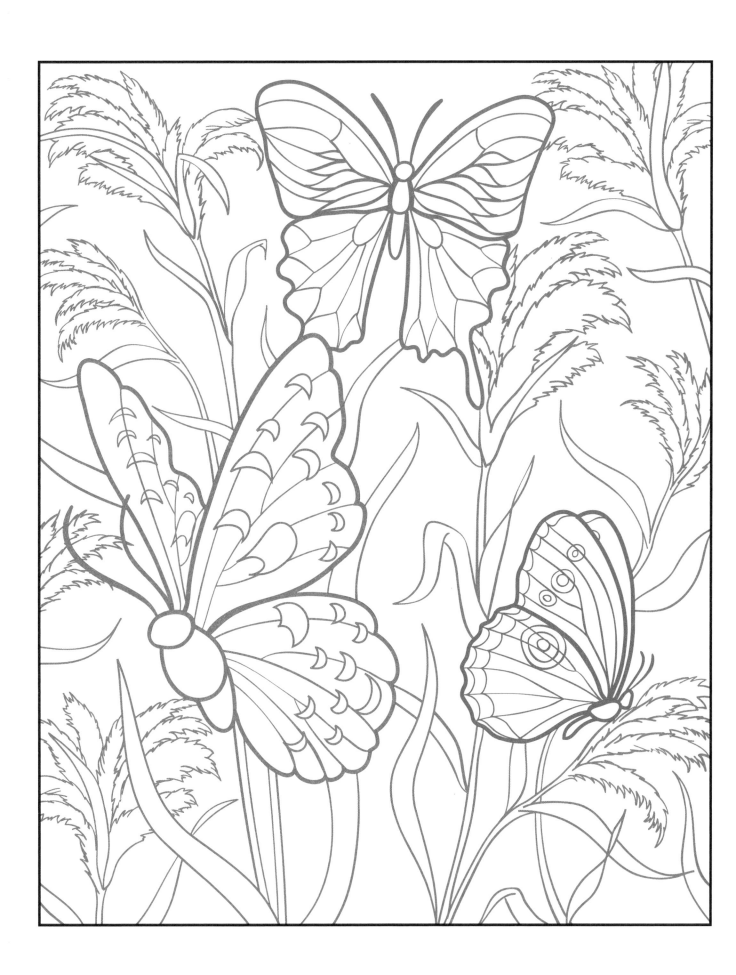

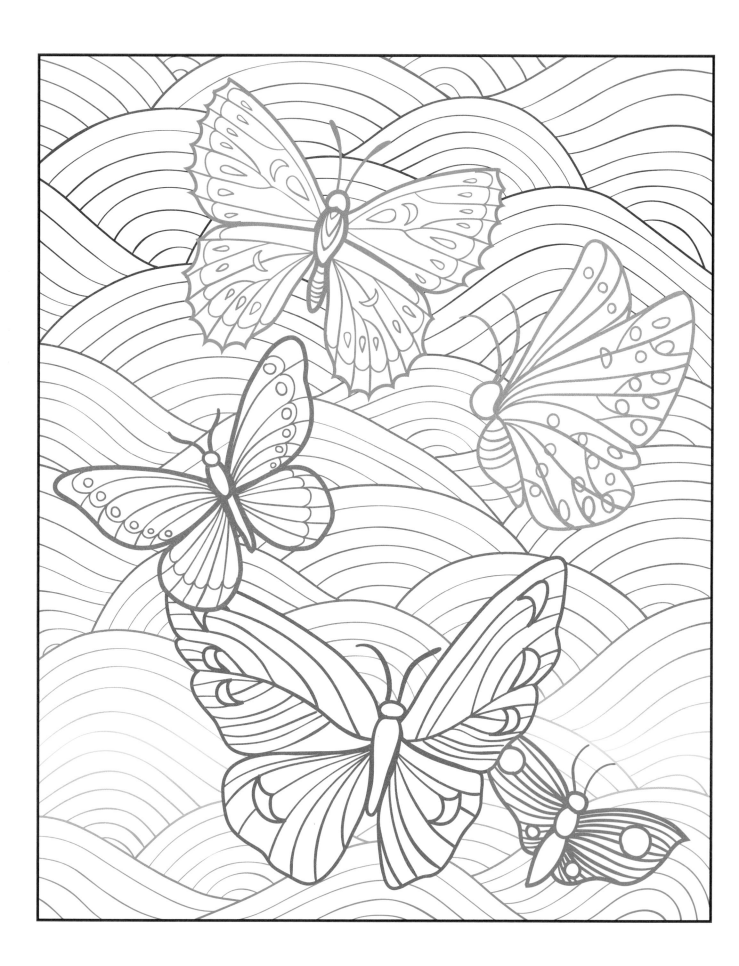

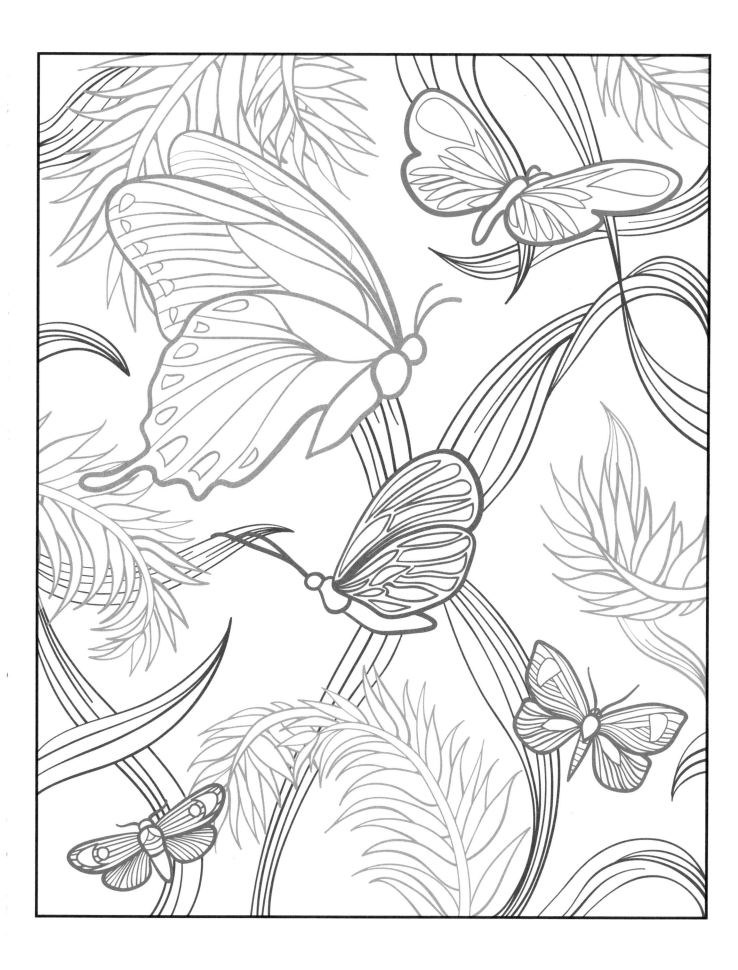

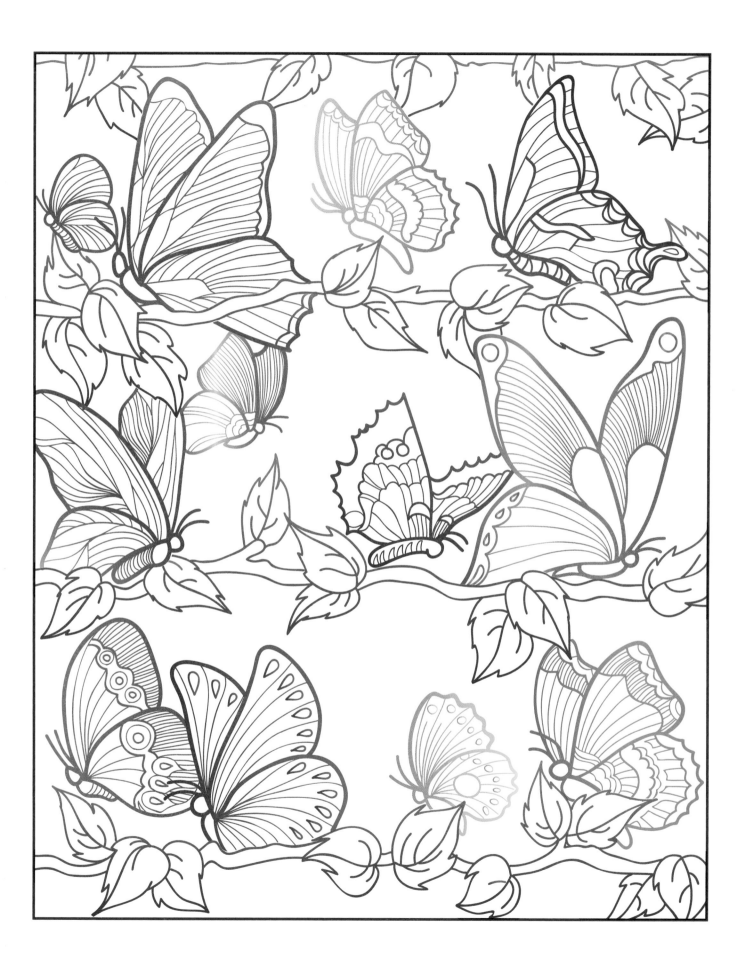

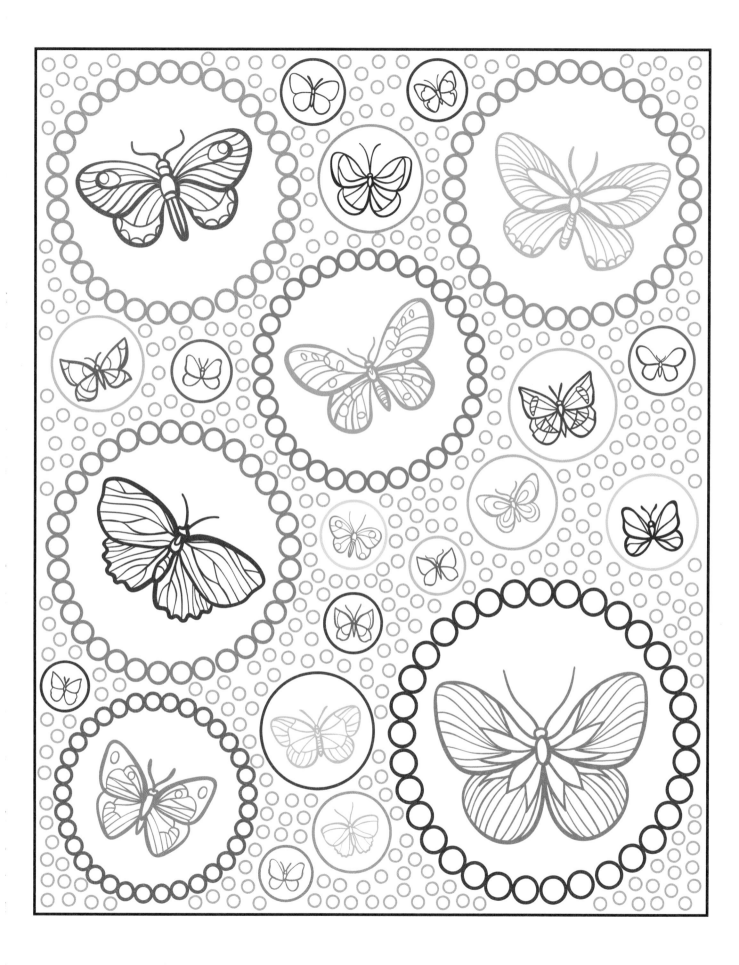

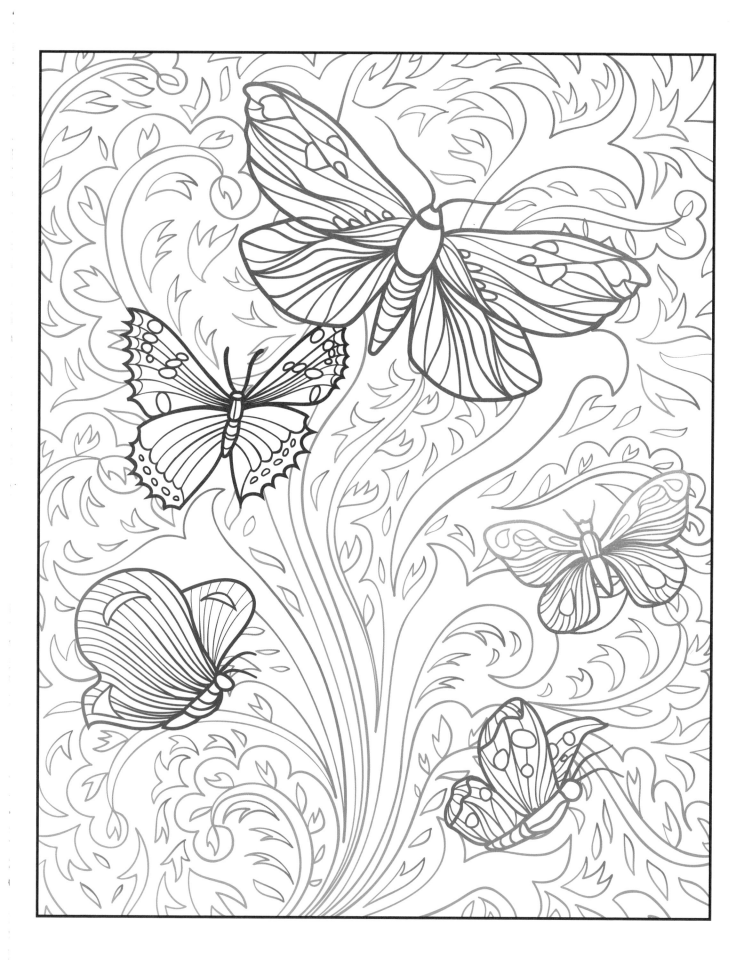

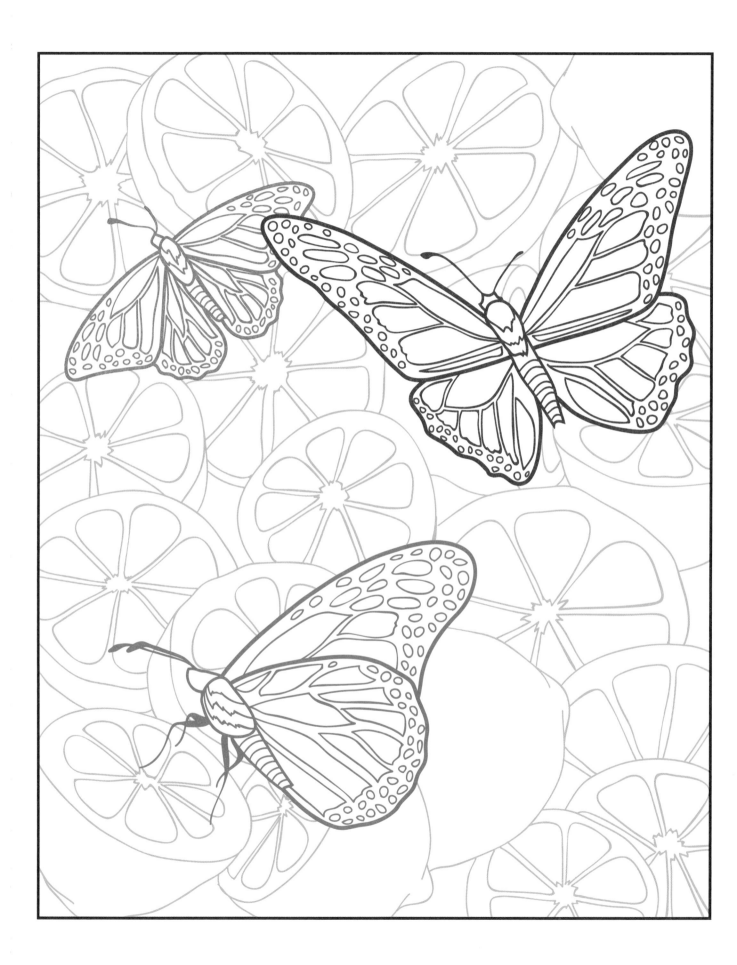

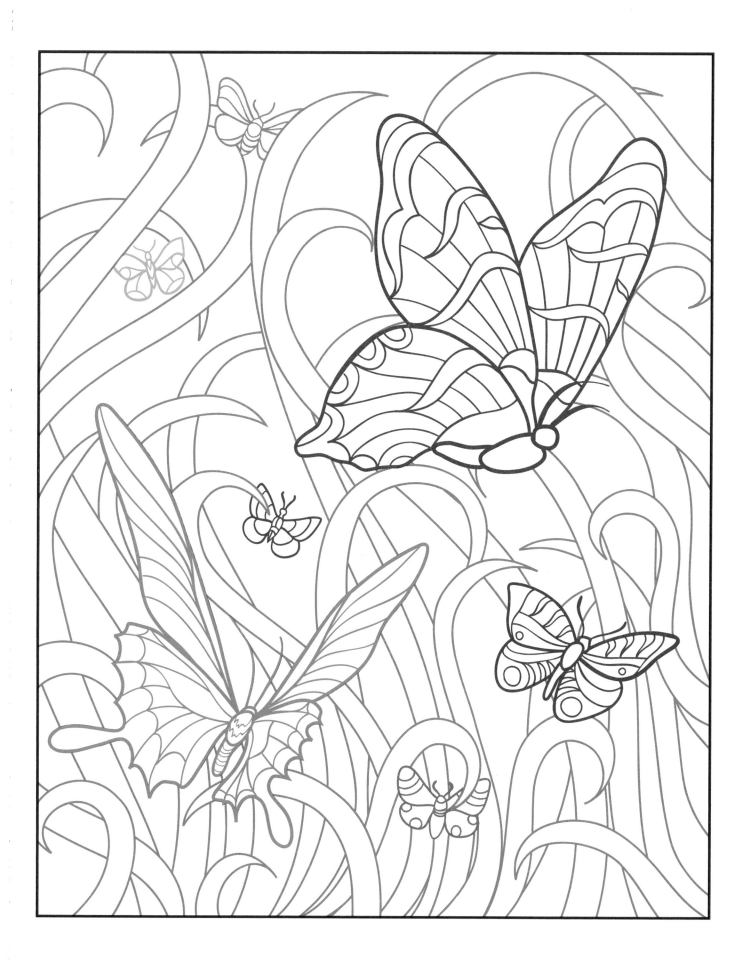

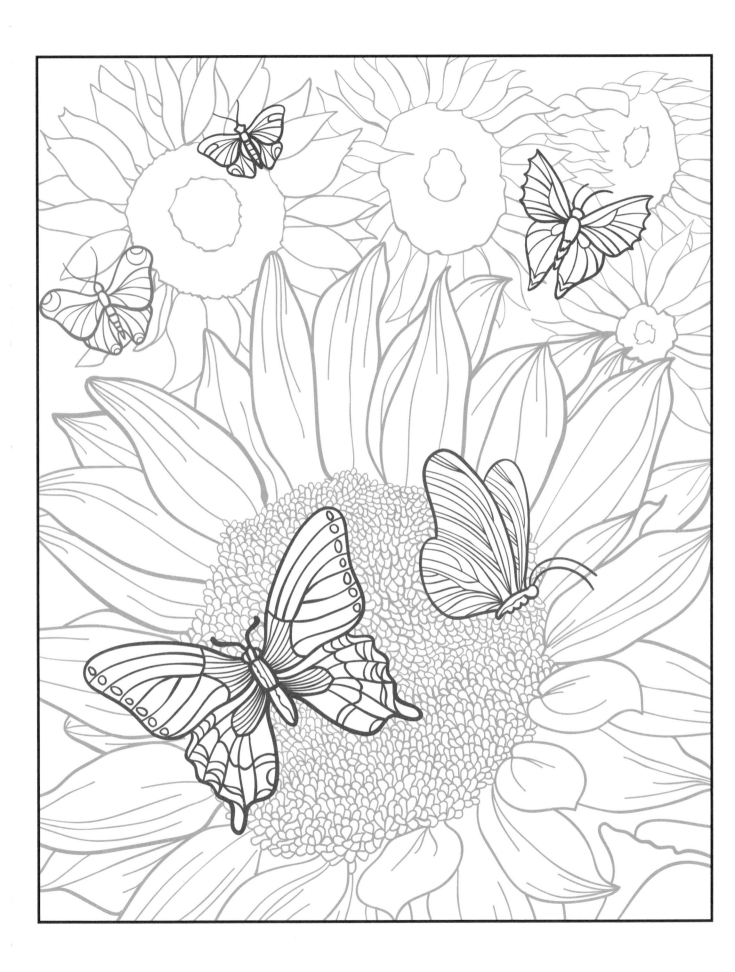

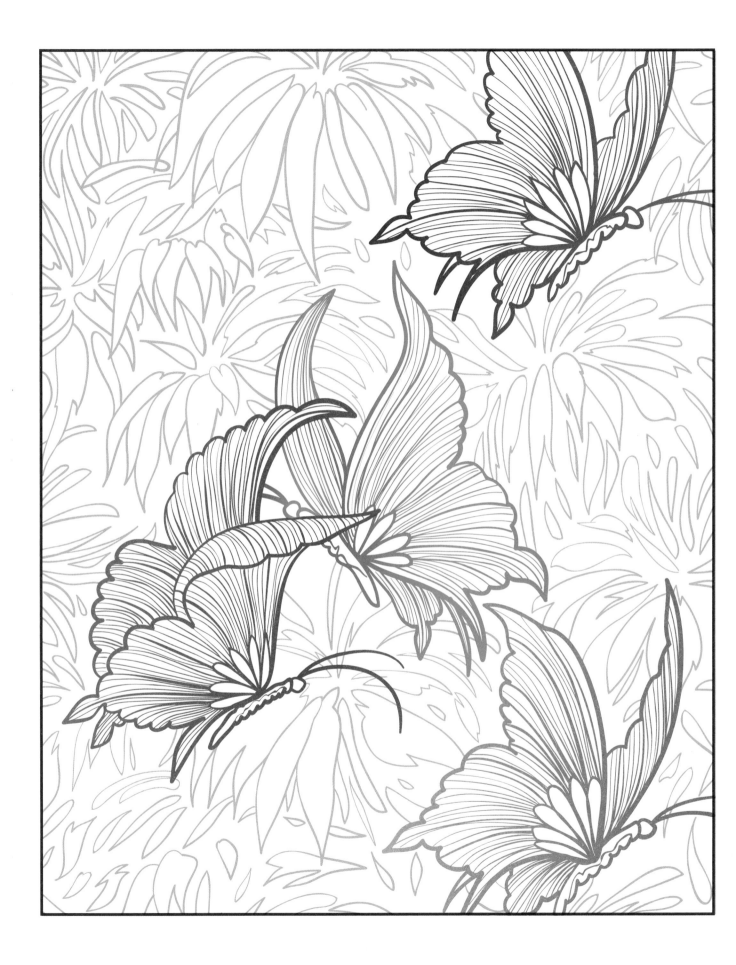

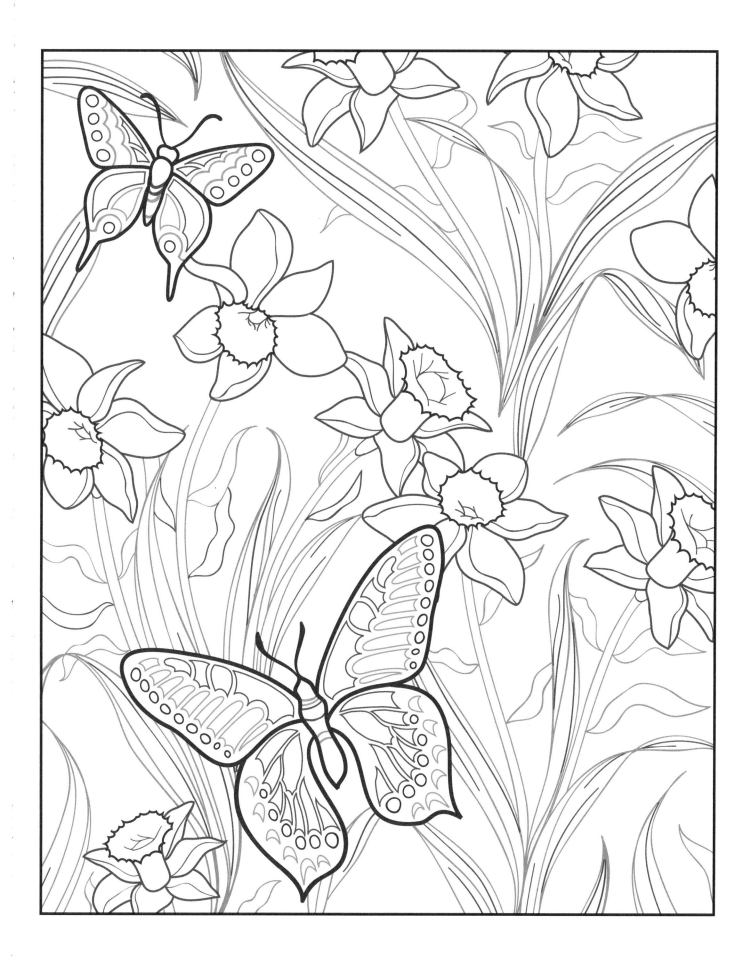

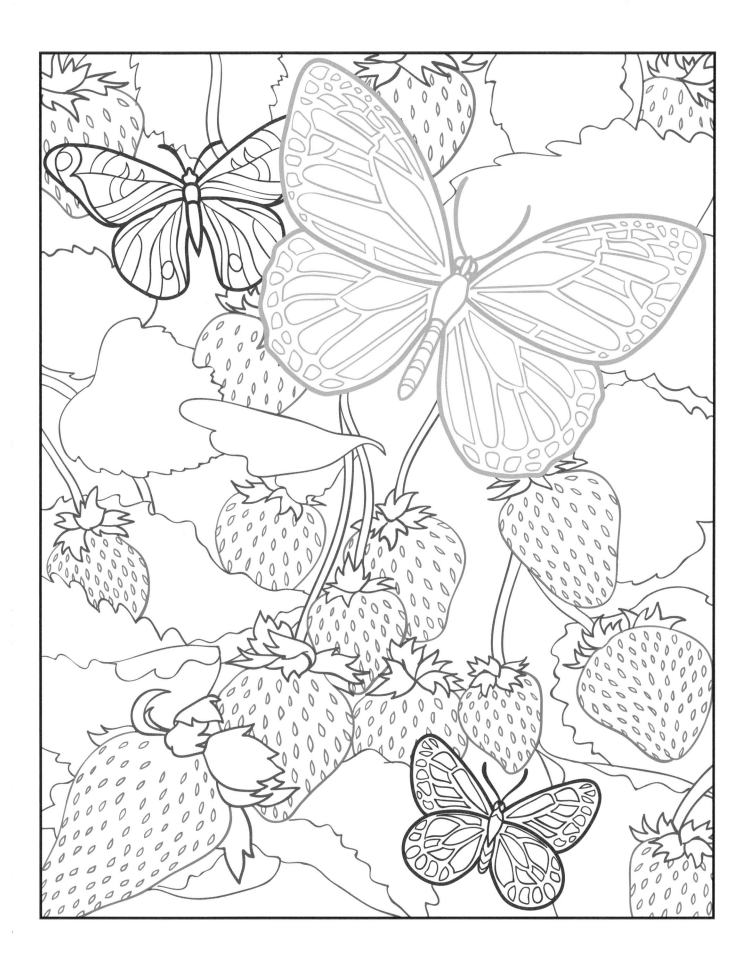

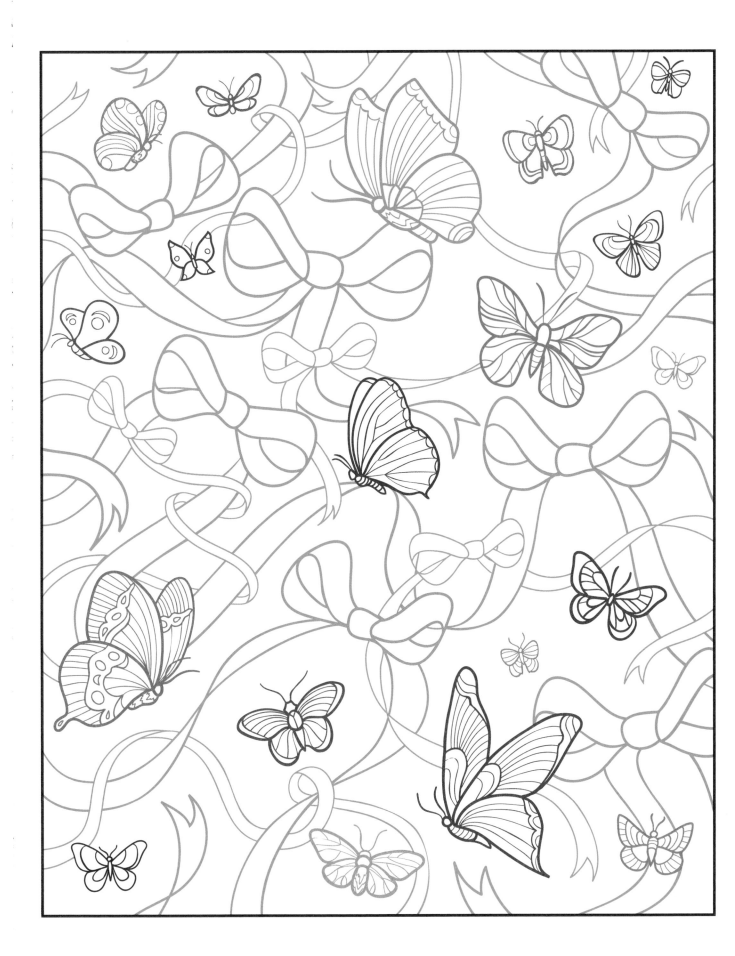

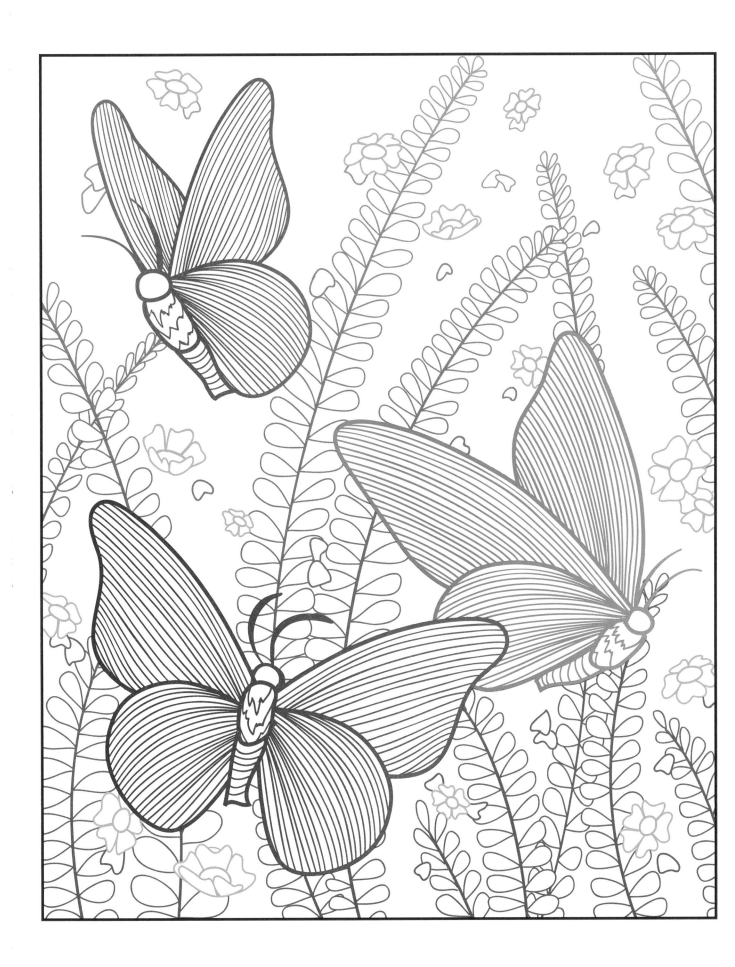

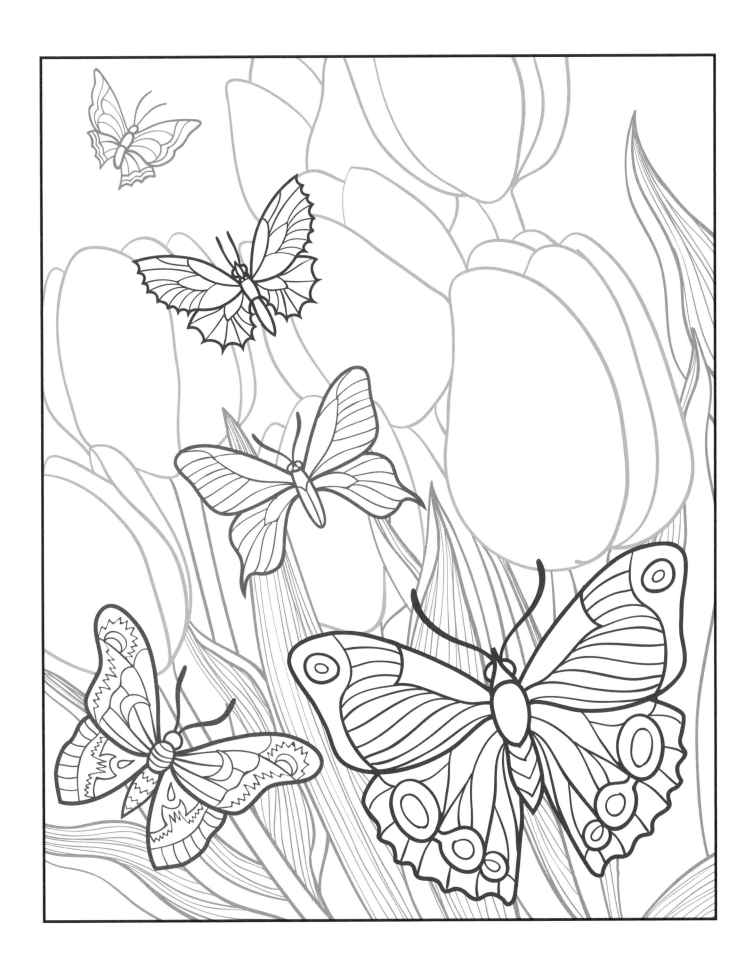

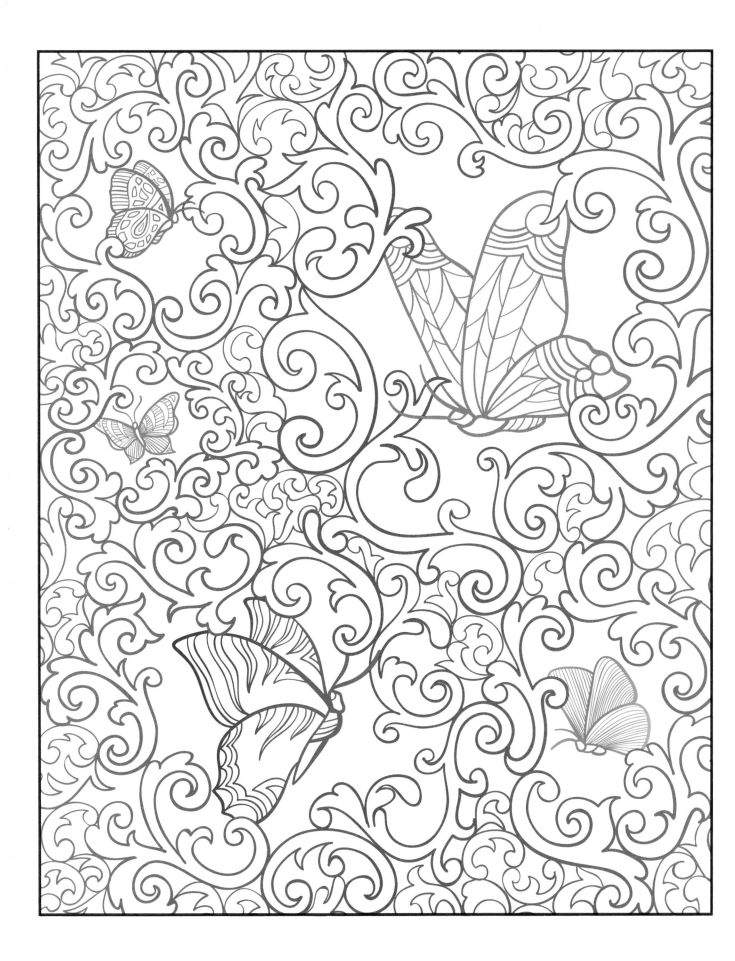

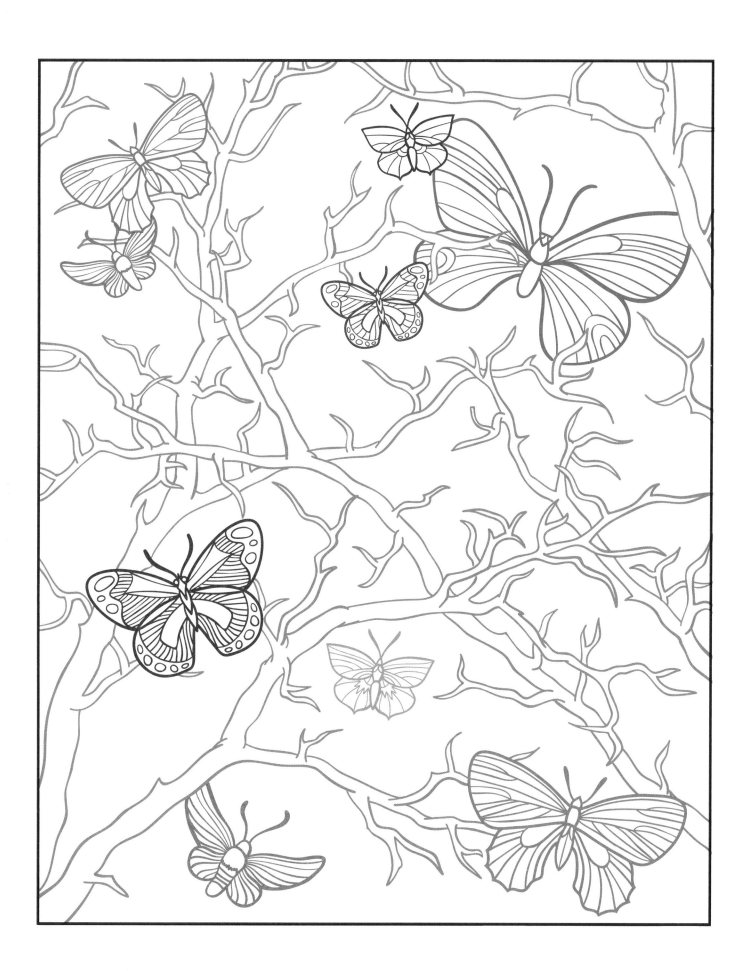

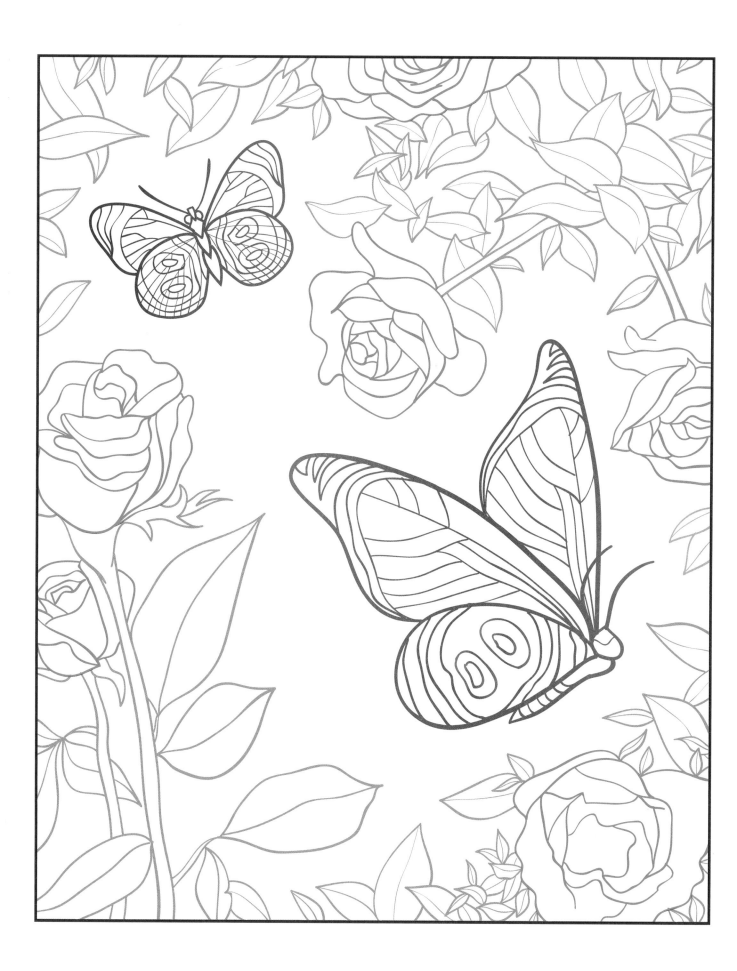

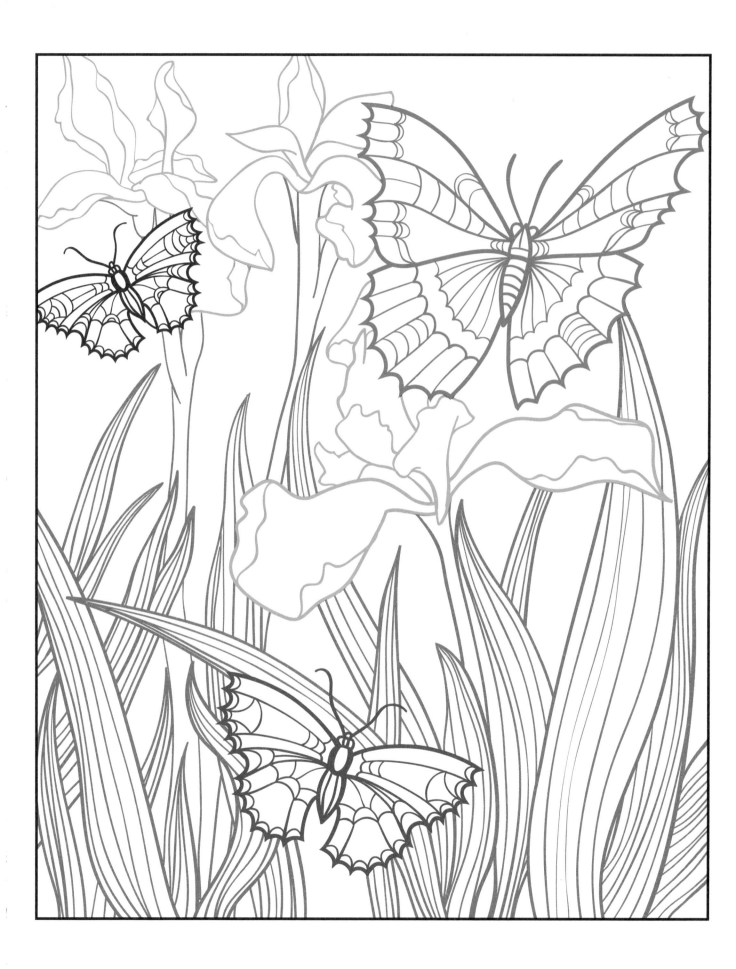

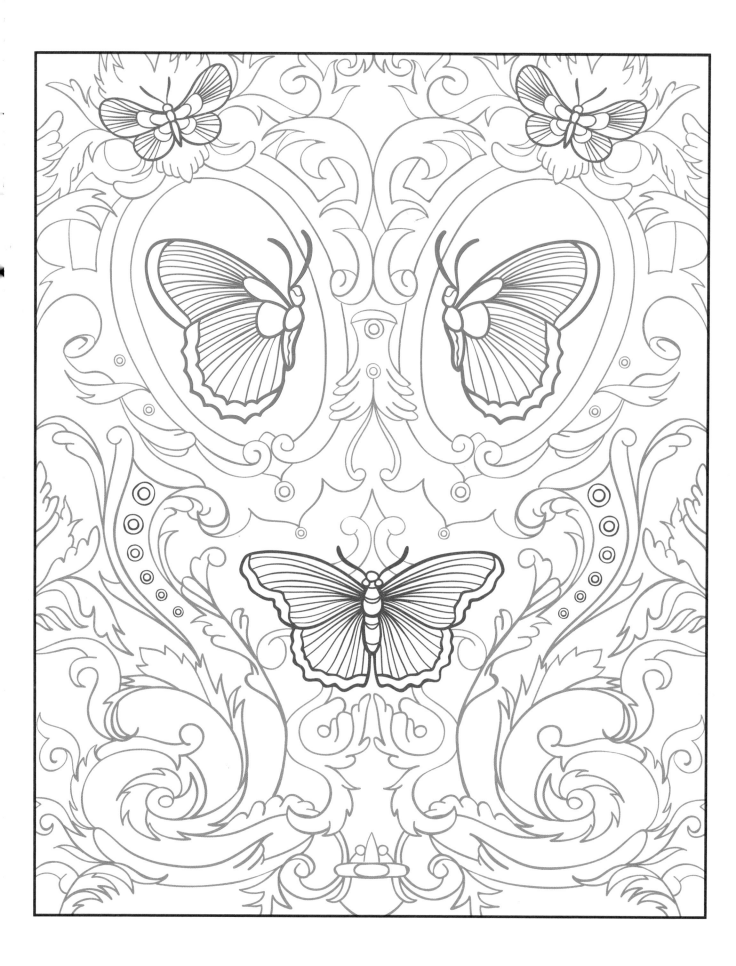

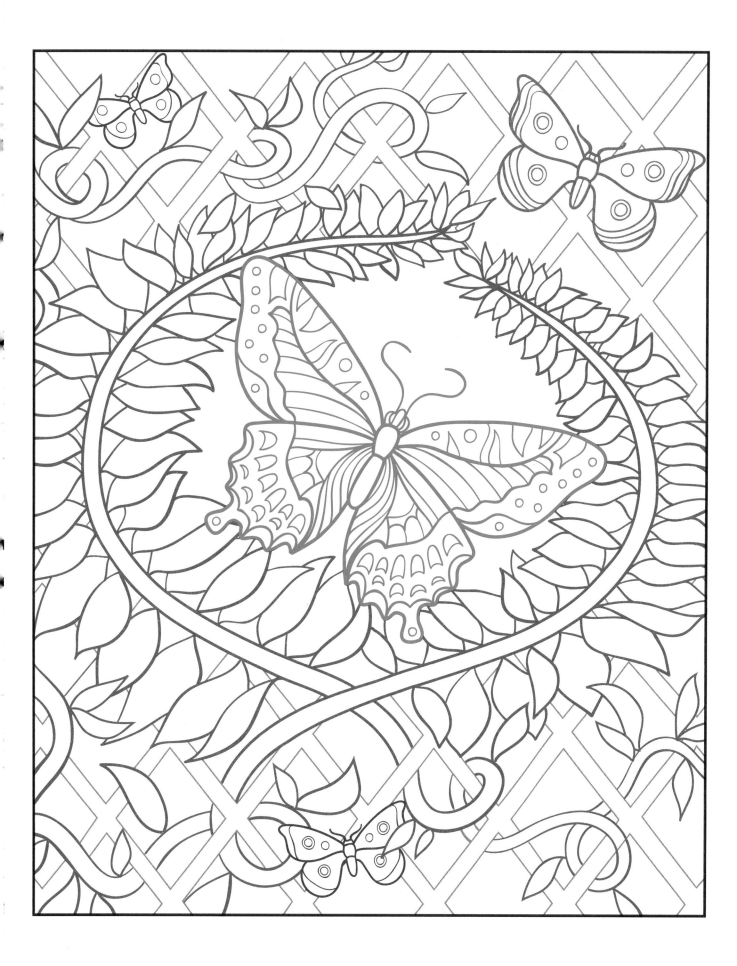